Creative Therapy

52 Exercises for Individuals and Groups

Jane Dossick & Eugene Shea

Illustrated by Eugene Shea

Professional Resource Press
Sarasota, Florida

Published by Professional Resource Press
(An imprint of Professional Resource Exchange, Inc.)
Post Office Box 15560
Sarasota, FL 34277-1560

This book was produced in the U.S.A. using a unique binding method that allows pages to lie flat for photocopying, is stronger than standard bindings for this purpose, and has numerous advantages over spiralbinding (e.g., less chance of damage in shipping, no unsightly spiral marks on photocopies, and a spine you can read when the book is on your bookshelf).

The copyeditor for this book was Patricia Rockwood, the managing editor was Debra Fink, the production coordinator was Laurie Girsch, and the cover designer was Stacey Sanders.

Library of Congress Cataloging-in-Publication Data

Dossick, Jane, date.
   Creative therapy : 52 exercises for individuals and groups / Jane Dossick & Eugene
Shea ; illustrated by Eugene Shea.
      p. cm.
   Includes bibliographical references (p.   ).
   ISBN-13: 978-1-56887-103-5 (alk. paper)
   ISBN-10: 1-56887-103-1 (alk. paper)
      1. Group psychotherapy--Problems, exercises, etc. I. Shea, Eugene, date. II. Title.

RC488.D672 2006
616.89'165--dc22

                                                                  2006040616

For Joanne, Philip, Stephanie, Kimberly, Stephen, and Carrie

TABLE OF CONTENTS

INTRODUCTION

WHO SHOULD USE THIS BOOK?

Like its predecessors, *Creative Therapy: 52 Exercises for Groups, Creative Therapy II: 52 More Exercises for Groups,* and *Creative Therapy III: 52 More Exercises for Groups*, this book has been designed as a practical guide to assist psychotherapists, group leaders, and specially trained teachers in mental health facilities, nursing homes, day programs, inpatient psychiatric units, special education programs, and support groups. It may be used as an adjunct to the psychotherapeutic treatment of such varied problems as Alzheimer's disease, schizophrenia, mental retardation, and depression.

The huge success of *Creative Therapy I, II,* and *III* led to the development of this sequel, which contains 52 new therapeutic exercises complete with illustrations that may be photocopied for group members. The exercises serve as an avenue to therapeutic discussions of important issues that might not be shared through other techniques.

Additionally, we have received feedback regarding the use of these exercises as part of the individual treatment of children. We have learned that children may enjoy the exercises and are consequently less inhibited about sharing fears, concerns, and fantasies. We have added recommendations to many of the exercises that may be adapted for use in individual sessions with children and adolescents, as well as adults.

As in the previous three works, this new book explains methods of energizing a group and takes both new and experienced group leaders through the stages for effective implementation of structured exercises. We find that these exercises can help group members and individuals develop interactive skills, motivate less-verbal individuals to contribute to discussions, and encourage group cohesiveness.

WHAT IS IN THIS BOOK?

Creative Therapy: 52 Exercises for Individuals and Groups is presented in an uncomplicated fashion so that the exercises will be nonthreatening to group members. The format allows the leader to refer to directions for each meeting and to photocopy the accompanying illustration, which becomes each member's worksheet. In each exercise, members complete a picture that focuses on a particular theme. A discussion follows in which the members discuss what their completed pictures reveal about themselves. Each member is able to look at his or her own illustration and express an initial response that might otherwise have been forgotten. The illustrations are intentionally simple to encourage participants to express themselves as freely as possible.

HOW DO YOU USE THIS BOOK?

Creative Therapy: 52 Exercises for Individuals and Groups combines the structured expression of art groups with the therapeutic communication of verbal discussion groups. The worksheet provided with each exercise serves as a springboard to discussion. Each exercise is accompanied by a step-by-step set of instructions for the group leader and therapist. Group members sit at a table, preferably in a circle. The leader hands out photocopies of the chosen exercises to members at the beginning of the session. The leader should seek to involve members immediately by asking about the picture.

The group leader introduces the theme, describes the exercise according to the instructions that accompany each drawing, and asks for feedback and comments from the group members. This initial discussion should be used to prepare the members for the task that follows.

Next, group members are given a time frame and directed to "fill in" or complete the exercise with their responses. Additional supplies such as crayons, markers, pens, or pencils may be handed out at this time.

It is important to be certain that everyone has a clear understanding of the task. If questions arise, it is recommended that members be encouraged to ask each other to paraphrase the instructions. In this way, members become actively involved and discover they can be helpful to one another.

Setting up a time frame is an important aspect of the structured exercise. These projects work best if the group members or individuals understand how much time is set aside for drawing or writing, and how much time is for discussion. For example, in a 1-hour session, 20 minutes might be used for explanation and drawing or writing, and 40 minutes for discussion.

These exercises should be nonthreatening. To reduce anxiety, group leaders should explain that content is more important than artistic talent, and that the drawings and writings are used simply to promote discussion. Some members may be resistant to drawing because of self-consciousness or physical limitations. Encouragement is helpful, but too much encouragement may become stressful. An alternative is to avoid adding extra pressure by allowing anxious members to write rather than draw their interpretations.

Group discussion immediately follows the drawing/writing period. The leader states a few minutes ahead of time when this will take place. Once group discussion begins, all members' comments should then be directed to the group as a whole.

Members are asked to volunteer to discuss their interpretations. The leader becomes a catalyst to promote and encourage verbal interaction and help focus the discussion. As members see one another present and receive feedback, more may volunteer to discuss their work.

WHAT ARE THE BENEFITS?

Projective art tasks introduce ideas that provide encouragement to groups searching for a common theme (Dalley, 1984). In addition, these structured exercises have a variety of other uses: to initiate members into a group process; as a warm-up technique; to help a group work through a particular stage in its development; to enhance group members' abilities to interact and share freely; to focus on a specific group need; and to help reduce the anxiety and uncertainty of group members and individuals. For example, if used with children, the exercises allow the child to indirectly or directly express important ideas, fantasies, and feelings. Significant information about family members and dynamics are often shared as a result of this approach. It must be understood, however, that these techniques are intended as a tool – as one part of a total approach to meet the goals of a particular group or individual sessions.

Structured exercises are a way of accelerating group interaction. Getting in touch with suppressed emotions helps the group as a whole as well as the individual members. Specific exercises may be chosen to help the group work through a particular problem (Hansen, Warner, & Smith, 1980).

Yalom (1983) describes the use of structured exercises with lower-level, inpatient psychotherapy groups. These groups often consist of members with a limited attention span, fearfulness, and confusion. Structured exercises may help such members express themselves. The use of drawing and writing exercises is especially helpful in fostering self-expression. These exercises may also stimulate group interest and provide variety. We believe the exercises in *Creative Therapy: 52 Exercises for Individuals and Groups* are very effective with this type of group.

Structured exercises also help ensure that no one dominates and that everyone has an opportunity to speak. A balance of verbal input is created. Monopolistic members must develop self-control to allow other members to have their turns. Shy or nonverbal members profit from the required participation, such as described by Levin and Kurtz (1974). These authors studied the effects of structured exercises in human relations groups and concluded that the inactive person benefits from a change in behavioral expectations. Greater opportunity for participation generates more ego-involvement, self-perceived personality changes, and increased group unity.

How does group therapy help group members? Feedback from one's peers, if properly channeled, can be a potent therapeutic force, promoting qualitative changes in self-expression, growth toward self-actualization, and changes in interpersonal behavior.

In his classic work on group psychotherapy, Yalom identifies key curative factors associated with the group process. We believe that many of the exercises included in *Creative Therapy: 52 Exercises for Individuals and Groups* facilitate the curative process. Generally, the exercises encourage sharing and development of trust among group members. The drawings illustrate common fears and anxieties and allow group members to see how they share many of the same concerns. Through the use of the illustrations, members are encouraged to support each other in finding solutions to problems and learn to support each other's needs. Skilled therapists will use the exercises strategically to support the development of other curative factors within the group.

WHAT ARE THE LIMITATIONS OF THESE EXERCISES?

Through experience, we have found these exercises and materials to be of great value. It is important, however, to realize the limitations of their use. As we have said, these exercises are to be used as a springboard to discussion and as an adjunct to other therapies.

Yalom (1985) describes possible negative effects structured exercises can have on groups. He suggests, for example, that they can create an atmosphere where critical stages of group interaction may be passed over. Structured exercises may also plunge the group members into sharing significant negative and positive feelings too quickly. In addition, the group leader may be too heavily relied upon by the members. This dissipates a group's potential effectiveness as a therapeutic agent.

The Lieberman, Yalom, and Miles encounter group project (1973) studied how structured exercises influence groups. The leaders who used relatively large numbers of structured exercises with their groups were often more popular with group members. However, group members were found to have a significantly lower outcome level than members participating in groups using fewer structured exercises.

There must be a balance to the use of structured exercises. The degree to which they should be used must be carefully weighed by the group leader; otherwise the leader runs the risk of reducing the group's potential and infantilizing the members. Some factors that determine the amount and type of structuring to be employed are the type of group, member characteristics, and the leaders' theoretical orientation (M. S. Corey & G. Corey, 1987).

Additionally, the group leader should keep in mind three of the considerations noted by Pfeiffer and Jones (1983). First, structured exercises should address the specific goals and purposes of the group. The leader should choose exercises directed at interests, concerns, or problems of individual members or of the group as a whole. Second, a more than casual understanding of the members is important, because revelation and exploration of fantasy can be threatening and anxiety provoking. Less-threatening exercises are recommended for groups with anxious or guarded members to promote openness rather than defensiveness. Third, different issues surface at various stages of group development. Groups will function best when the level of feedback expected corresponds to the developmental stage of the group. In early stages of group development, exercises that focus on openness and building trust are more appropriate. Exercises that focus on critical feedback and appraisal will be more successful in the later stages of group development. When used in individual sessions with children, adolescents, or adults, these exercises should only be considered one part of the total therapeutic approach.

CONCLUSION

Creative Therapy: 52 Exercises for Individuals and Groups should offer rewarding experiences for both group leaders and group members. The structured exercises in this book make it easier for group members to focus ideas, feelings, and experiences related to the topic of discussion. Members further benefit from revealing themselves, exchanging feedback, and supporting one another emotionally.

The purpose of this book, however, is first and foremost to help group leaders, therapists, and teachers conduct their groups by providing a framework for successful group experiences. Through the use of specific suggestions, we describe the procedures necessary for group leaders to handle the widest variety of group therapy applications.

In addition, the use of these exercises may also help to alert group leaders to issues for further exploration in individual counseling or other group therapies. Although designed primarily for groups, with slight modification many of these exercises can be used in individual treatment for children, adolescents, and adults.

REFERENCES

Corey, M. S., & Corey, G. (1987). *Groups: Process & Practice* (3rd ed.). Monterey, CA: Brooks/ Cole.

Dalley, T. (1984). *Art as Therapy: An Introduction to the Use of Art as a Therapeutic Technique.* New York: Tavistock.

Hansen, J. C., Warner, R. W., & Smith, E. J. (1980). *Group Counseling: Theory and Process* (2nd ed.). Chicago: Rand McNally.

Levin, E. N., & Kurtz, R. R. (1974). Structured and non structured human relations training. *Journal of Counseling Psychology, 21,* 526-531.

Lieberman, M. A., Yalom, I. D., & Miles, M. B. (1973). *Encounter Groups: First Facts.* New York: Basic Books.

Pfeiffer, J. W., & Jones, J. E. (1983). *A Handbook of Structured Experiences for Human Relations Training: Reference Guide to Handbooks and Annuals.* San Diego: University Associates.

Yalom, I. D. (1983). *Inpatient Group Psychotherapy.* New York: Basic Books.

Yalom, I. D. (1985). *The Theory and Practice of Group Psychotherapy* (3rd ed.). New York: Basic Books.

Creative Therapy

52 Exercises for Individuals and Groups

Exercise 1

LOST IN THE CROWD

Question:

What does it mean to feel alone?

Draw or Write:

In the blank space in the middle of the crowd, draw or write about a time in your life when you were with other people but still felt alone.

To Talk About:

- What are some of the reasons you felt so alone?
- Did someone do or say something to provoke your feelings of loneliness?
- Can you think of something you might have done to feel less alone?
- Is there someone you might be able to help to feel less lonely?

Recommendations:

This exercise may be useful in individual sessions with children, adolescents, and adults, as well as groups in the middle to later stages of development whose members are well acquainted with one another.

Exercise 2

THE PRIVACY ISSUE

Question:

Why should we respect each other's privacy?

Draw a Circle:

Circle places in the illustration where some privacy might be needed. Draw "X's" in the illustration where privacy is required.

To Talk About:

- Describe the parts of the room you chose to circle and marked with an "X."
- Describe your feelings when other people do not consider your privacy to be important.
- Suggest ways that would help others to respect your privacy.

Recommendations:

This exercise may be useful in individual sessions with children, adolescents, and adults. It may also be effective in a variety of group settings with groups in all stages of development.

Exercise 3

OH NO – ANOTHER ARGUMENT

Question:

How does it make you feel when people you know are having an argument?

Draw or Write:

Color in everyone who might be involved in a particular dispute. Illustrate (or write) what this argument is about.

To Talk About:

- Describe this argument. How did it start?
- How do each of the people arguing feel?
- Can you suggest a way to end this argument?
- What might people do to make it less likely they'll get into future arguments?

Recommendations:

This exercise may be useful in individual sessions with children and adolescents. It may also be effective with groups in all stages of group development.

Exercise 4

A NEW FRIEND

Question:

What are some of the ways in which people become friends?

Draw or Write:

Fill in all the clothing on both figures, and illustrate a good friend of yours, and yourself. Color in the words that best describe what qualities are important to you in a friend.

To Talk About:

- Was there a reason you dressed the people that particular way?
- Describe the words you have colored in.
- Why are these things important to you in a friend?
- Would your life change if you had a friend like this?
- Describe how your life would be different.

Recommendations:

This exercise may be useful in individual sessions with children, adolescents, and adults. It may also be effective in group settings in all stages of group development.

Exercise 5

NO TIME FOR ME

Questions:

1. How does it make you feel when people don't take you seriously and won't listen to your ideas?
2. What are some of the situations in which grownups seem too busy to notice you?

Draw or Write:

On the left side of the illustration, check off any thoughts and feelings you may have experienced. On the right side of the illustration, check off all the feelings you have experienced. Try to draw a face to go along with those feelings.

To Talk About:

- Describe how you feel about the situation in the picture.
- What should other people do to give you some of the attention you feel you need?

Recommendations:

This exercise may be useful in individual sessions with children and adolescents.

☐ "You Know who" gets
   more attention
☐ People think I am too young
   to say something important
☐ Adults are always too busy
   with something else

☐ unwanted
☐ lonely
☐ angry
☐ unimportant
☐ jealous
☐ sad

Exercise 6

THE TREASURE CHEST

Questions:

1. Can you think of different things that people may consider a treasure?
2. Is there something you wish you could have that would become your new treasure?

Draw or Write:

Above the picture of the treasure chest, draw or write about something you consider a treasure. It can be something you already have or wish you could have. Beside the picture of the man, draw anyone who you think could either help you get your treasure or appreciate why it is special to you.

To Talk About:

- Describe your treasure.
- Why did you choose it?
- Why did you choose that person or persons drawn beside you?
- What would some of your friends and family consider to be treasure(s)?

Recommendations:

This exercise may be effective in individual sessions with children, adolescents, and adults. It may also be useful in a variety of group settings with groups in all stages of development.

Exercise 7

SOME PLACES THAT MAKE US FEEL NERVOUS

Question:

How does it make you feel to be in places that make you nervous?

Draw or Write:

Put your name beneath the silhouette. Color in the places that might make you nervous. Complete the thought bubble.

To Talk About:

- Describe how each place you colored in makes you feel.
- Tell the reasons that being in those places makes you anxious or uncomfortable.
- Is there any way you could feel less anxious about these places?

Recommendations:

This exercise may be useful in individual sessions with children and adolescents.

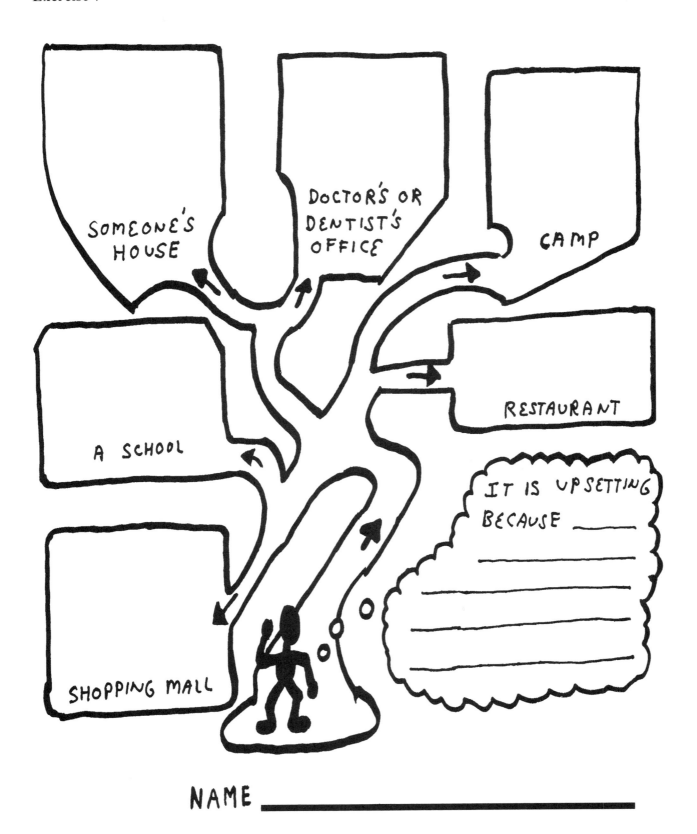

SOMEONE'S HOUSE

DOCTOR'S OR DENTIST'S OFFICE

CAMP

A SCHOOL

RESTAURANT

IT IS UPSETTING BECAUSE _____

SHOPPING MALL

NAME _____

Exercise 8

MOUNTAINS OUT OF MOLEHILLS

Question:

How does it make you feel when someone gets upset over a problem or situation that you think is really not a big deal?

Draw or Write:

On the molehill, draw or write a situation or problem that at first appeared to be small. On the mountain, draw or write how the situation got blown out of proportion.

To Talk About:

- Describe the situation that you thought was small, and why you thought it was not that big a deal.
- Describe how it was turned into a bigger problem than necessary.
- Can you suggest any way this problem could have been solved without it becoming such a big deal?

Recommendations:

This exercise may be useful in individual sessions with children, adolescents, and adults. It may also be effective with a variety of groups in all stages of development.

Exercise 9

MY LITTLE VILLAGE

Question:

What makes the area you live in seem important or special to you?

Draw or Write:

Pretend you are creating the "perfect town" with only four buildings in it. Choose a plot and design your own house. Design the other three as important buildings you would want in your town or neighborhood. Add any additional features you want, such as trees, railroads, cars, people, animals, or anything else. Use the lines at the bottom of the page to describe the town and some of the people who live there. Fill in the name of your town in the banner.

To Talk About:

- What is it you'd like people to know about the home you've created?
- Why did you choose the other buildings to add to your town or neighborhood?
- Who would you like living in this little village with you?
- What might be happening in each building you've created?

Recommendations:

This exercise may be effective in individual sessions with children, adolescents, and adults. It may also be effective with a wide variety of groups in all stages of development.

WELCOME TO
THE TOWN OF

Exercise 10

CRISIS AND CHANGE

Question:

What does it mean to be in a crisis?

Draw or Write:

In the crisis area, draw or write about a troubling situation in your life. Check off the box that best describes how you responded to the situation.

To Talk About:

- Describe the crisis and how you responded.
- Why do you think you responded the way you did?
- What do you think influenced your actions or inactions?
- How did things turn out?

Recommendations:

This exercise may be effective in individual sessions with children, adolescents, and adults. It may also be useful in a variety of groups whose members are well acquainted with one another.

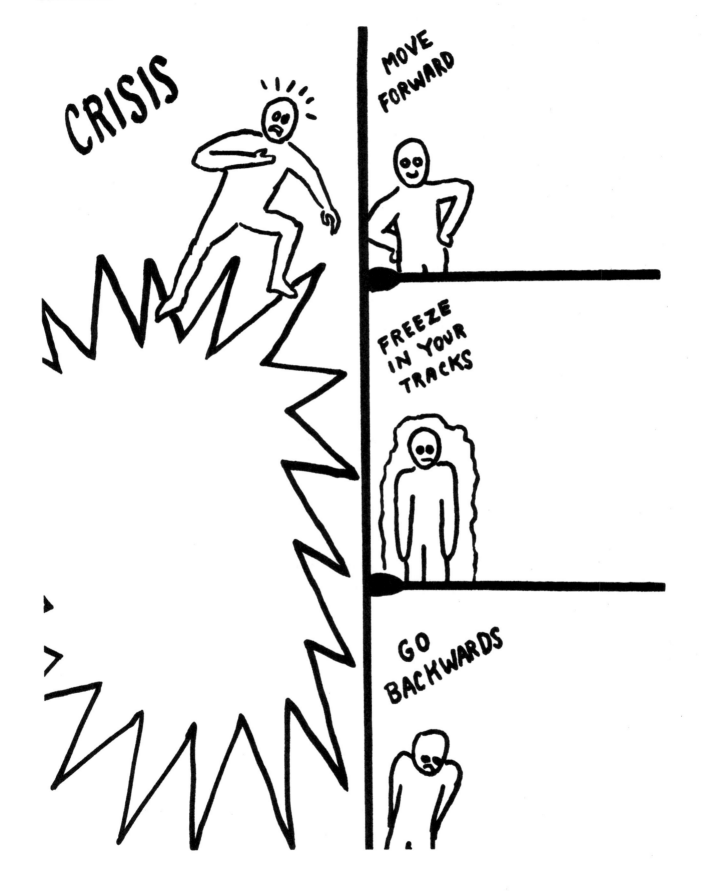

Exercise 11

GOALS WITHIN YOUR REACH

Question:

Why is it important not only to have goals, but to be able to plan how to reach them?

Draw or Write:

In the goal post, illustrate your goal. Along the way, draw or write some of the smaller steps you might take to reach your goal.

To Talk About:

- Talk about how realistic you think your goal is.
- Talk about all the steps you chose along the way to help you reach your goal.
- If you can't reach this goal, are there any other goals you could possibly substitute for it?

Recommendations:

This exercise may be effective in individual sessions with children, adolescents, and adults. It may also be useful in a variety of group settings with groups in all stages of group development.

GOAL POST

Exercise 12

NOT GETTING MY WAY

Question:

How do most people react when they want something and the answer is no?

Draw or Write:

In the blank box, write or draw a time when someone said no to you. You may use examples given, or come up with a situation of your own. You may write or draw it in the circle at the top of the page.

To Talk About:

- Describe the situation you wrote or illustrated.
- Can you remember a time you had to tell somebody else they couldn't have their way? What happened?
- What do you think would be the best way to handle these situations?

Recommendations:

This exercise may be useful in individual sessions with children and adolescents.

Exercise 13

MY DREAM HOUSE

Question:

Would the idea of designing your own house, inviting the guests, and planning activities in the rooms appeal to you?

Draw or Write:

Illustrate an activity in each room. Include the people who would enjoy participating in each room's activity. (You may use the same person in more than one room.) Draw at least one important object somewhere in your imaginary house.

To Talk About:

- Describe your dream house and what you have illustrated in each room.
- Why did you choose the people you did? Why did you have them participating in those activities?
- Is there any way you could change something about where you live to make it more like your dream house?

Recommendations:

This exercise may be useful in individual sessions with children, adolescents, and adults. It may also be effective in a variety of group settings, with groups in all stages of development.

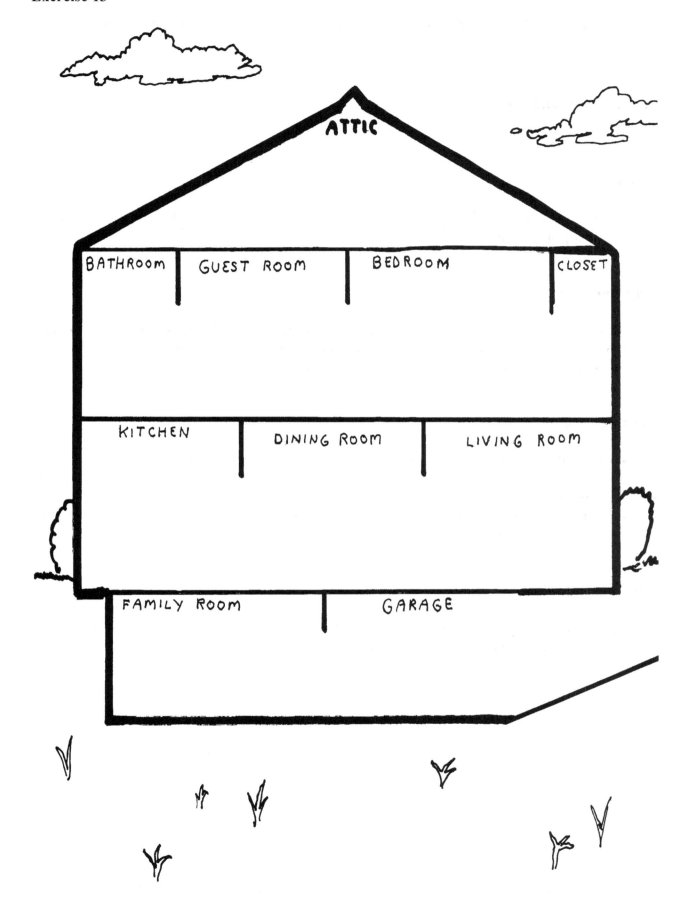

Exercise 14

SIBLINGS IN THE SPOTLIGHT

Questions:

1. What does it mean when someone is in the spotlight?
2. How does it feel to be left out of that spotlight, and not get a lot of attention?

Draw or Write:

In the circle beside the kid performing, draw a picture of your brother or sister or someone else close to you doing something that gets a lot of attention. Illustrate something in the thought bubble above the other child's head, to show how he or she may be reacting to this.

To Talk About:

- How do you feel when you watch this person get all the attention?
- What do you think the grownups should do?
- If the spotlight were on you, what would you do to get a lot of attention?
- Did this ever really happen?

Recommendations:

This exercise may be effective in individual sessions with children and adolescents.

Exercise 14

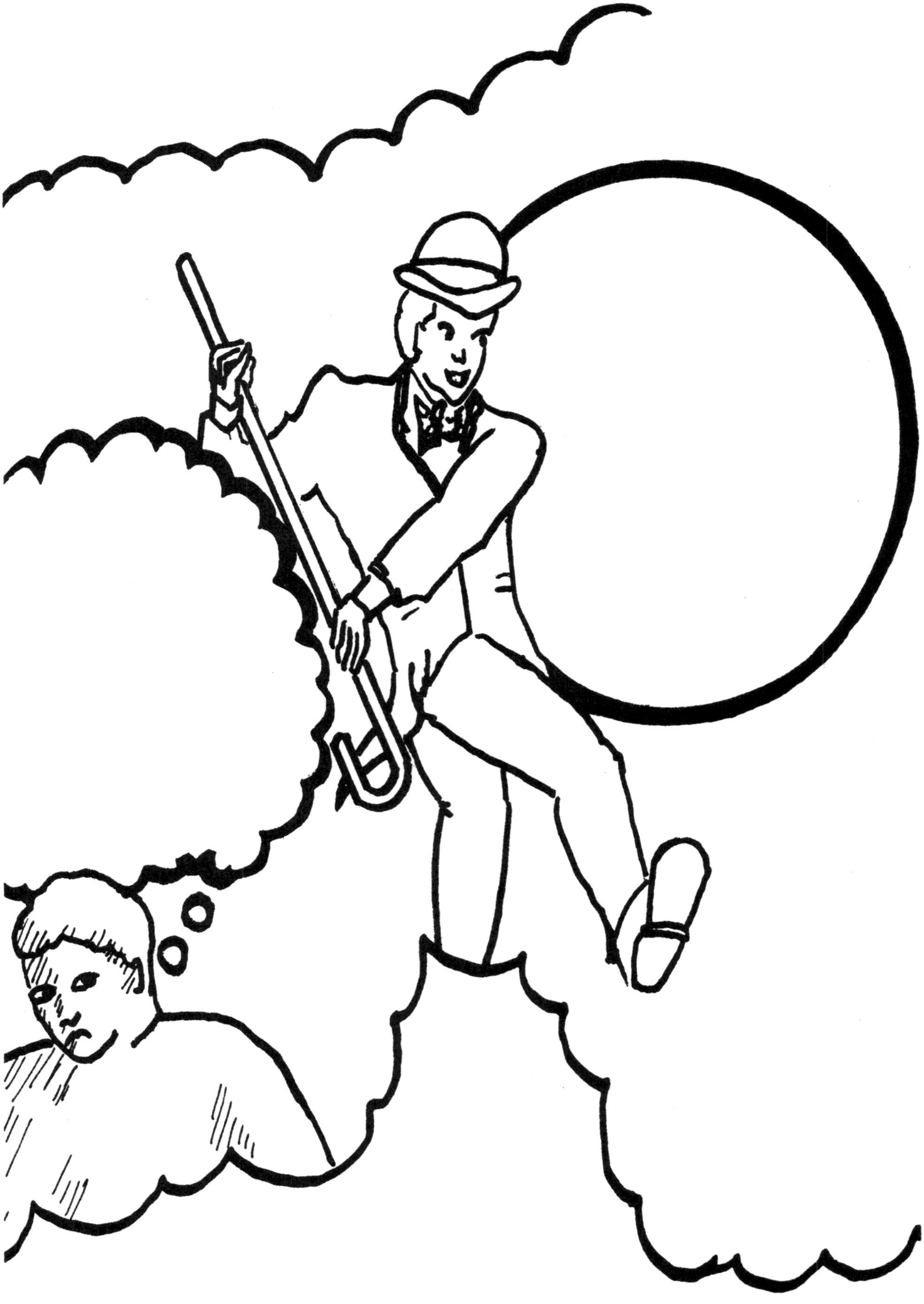

Exercise 15

IMAGINARY TIME TRAVEL

Question:

How do favorite memories from the past and dreams for the future make you feel?

Draw or Write:

- In the blank space on the left side of the page, imagine that you are back in time, and illustrate the best event that has already taken place in your life. How old were you when this event took place?
- Now, imagine that you are traveling into the future; on the right side of the page, illustrate a wonderful event you wish would take place in the future.

To Talk About:

- Describe both the past and future events you illustrated.
- What makes these events so meaningful for you?
- Is there anything you might do to increase the chances that the future event you illustrated could actually take place?

Recommendations:

This exercise may be effective in individual sessions with children, adolescents, and adults. It may also be useful in a variety of group settings with groups in all stages of group development.

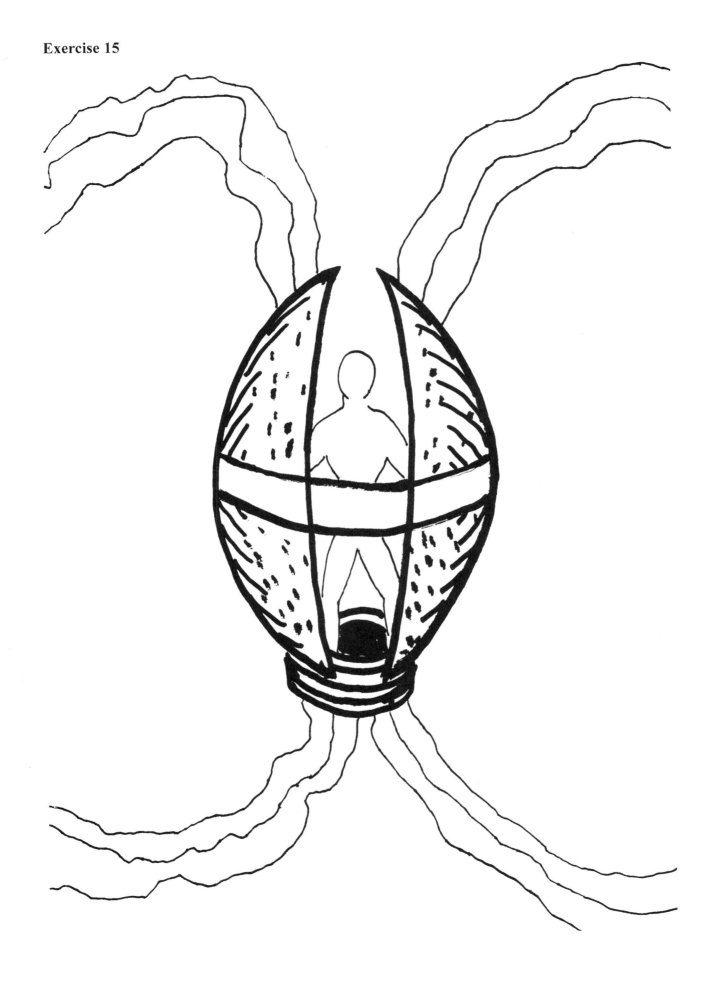

Exercise 16

A HELPING HAND

Question:

Why is it important for people to help each other?

Draw or Write:

In the appropriate circle, draw

- who the helper is.
- what type of help is being offered.
- who is being helped.

To Talk About:

- Describe what you drew in each circle.
- Give details about the situation in which some help was needed and given.
- Were you ever in a situation where you helped someone else?
- Describe any way that people you know could help each other more.

Recommendations:

This exercise may be useful in individual sessions with children, adolescents, and adults. It may also be useful in group settings in all stages of group development.

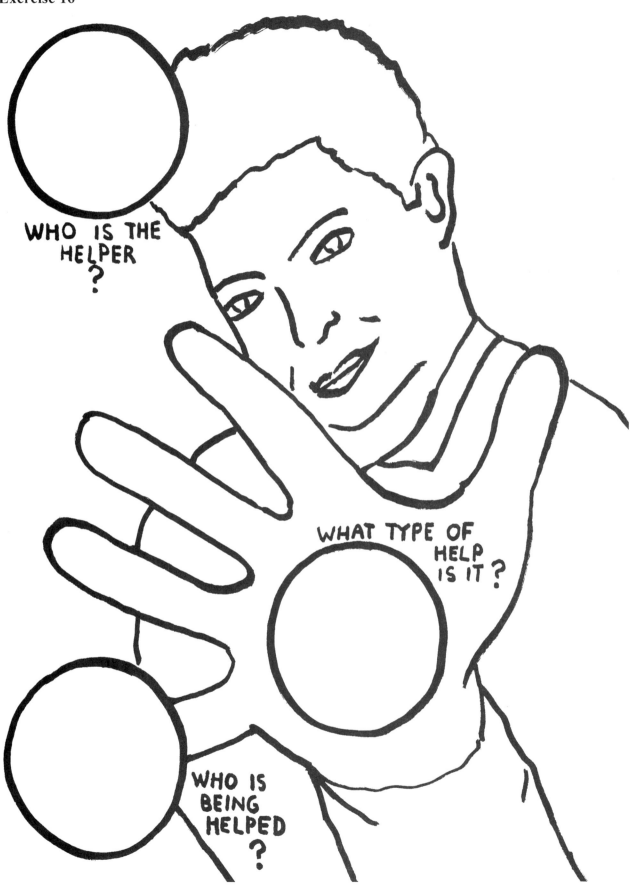

Exercise 17

THE SAFETY GAME

Question:

What are some dangerous things that could happen in places we go to, when we're not careful?

Draw or Write:

In each box, fill in safety tips for that place.

To Talk About:

- Describe the importance of the safety tips you illustrated.
- Are there any other safety tips you could add for your home or any other place you spend time in?

Recommendations:

This exercise may be useful in individual sessions with children and adolescents, as well as a variety of group settings with groups in all stages of development.

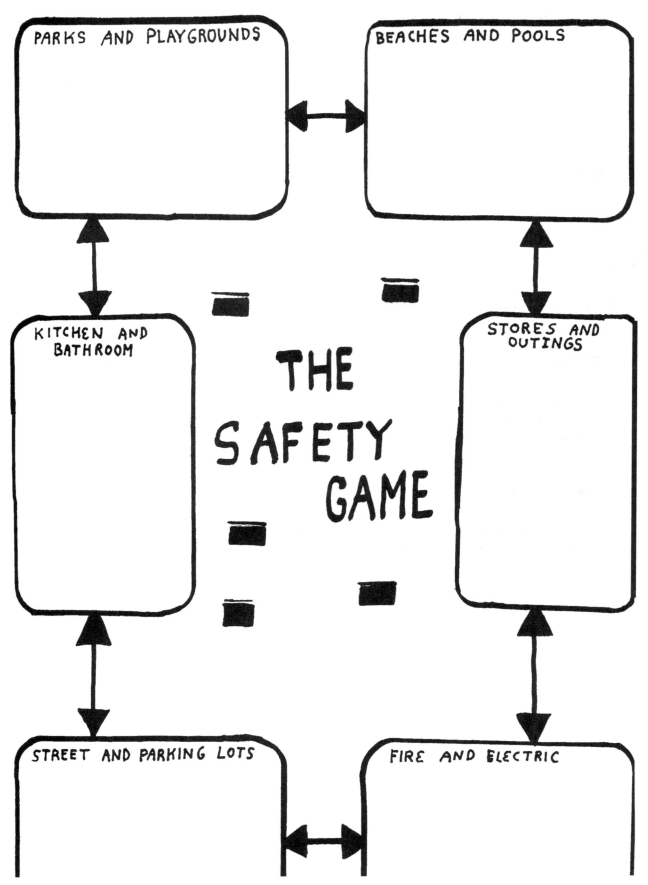

Exercise 18

LOOKING UP TO OTHERS

Question:

What does it mean to say, "You are my idol"?

Draw or Write:

On the illustration of the pedestal, draw someone you look up to. In the space provided below, write in the reasons you look up to this person.

To Talk About:

- Describe the person you admire and what it is that makes him or her seem special.
- Describe other reasons people might look up to someone.

Recommendations:

This exercise may be useful in individual sessions with children, adolescents, and adults. It may also be effective in a variety of group settings in all stages of development.

Exercise 19

CALENDAR OF SPECIAL EVENTS

Question:

How does it make you feel when you know something special is planned for a future date?

Draw or Write:

In a few of the months on the calendar or on the reminder notes below, illustrate some special events you would like to see take place.

To Talk About:

- Describe the special events you have illustrated.
- Is there anyone you would like to share these events with?
- Are there any events you do not look forward to?

Recommendations:

This exercise may be effective in individual sessions with children, adolescents, and adults. It may also be useful in a variety of group settings, with groups in all stages of development.

Exercise 20

A TALK SHOW

Question:

Why is it interesting to hear others share their opinions and feelings on television?

Draw or Write:

Fill in the host and guests in the illustrated chairs. (You may put yourself anywhere in the picture.) Include people you know in the audience.

To Talk About:

- Why did you choose those people to be guests and hosts?
- What is the topic everyone is talking about?
- Did you have any particular reason for including those people in the show?

Recommendations:

This exercise may be useful in individual sessions with children, adolescents, and adults. It may also be effective with a variety of groups in all stages of development.

Exercise 20

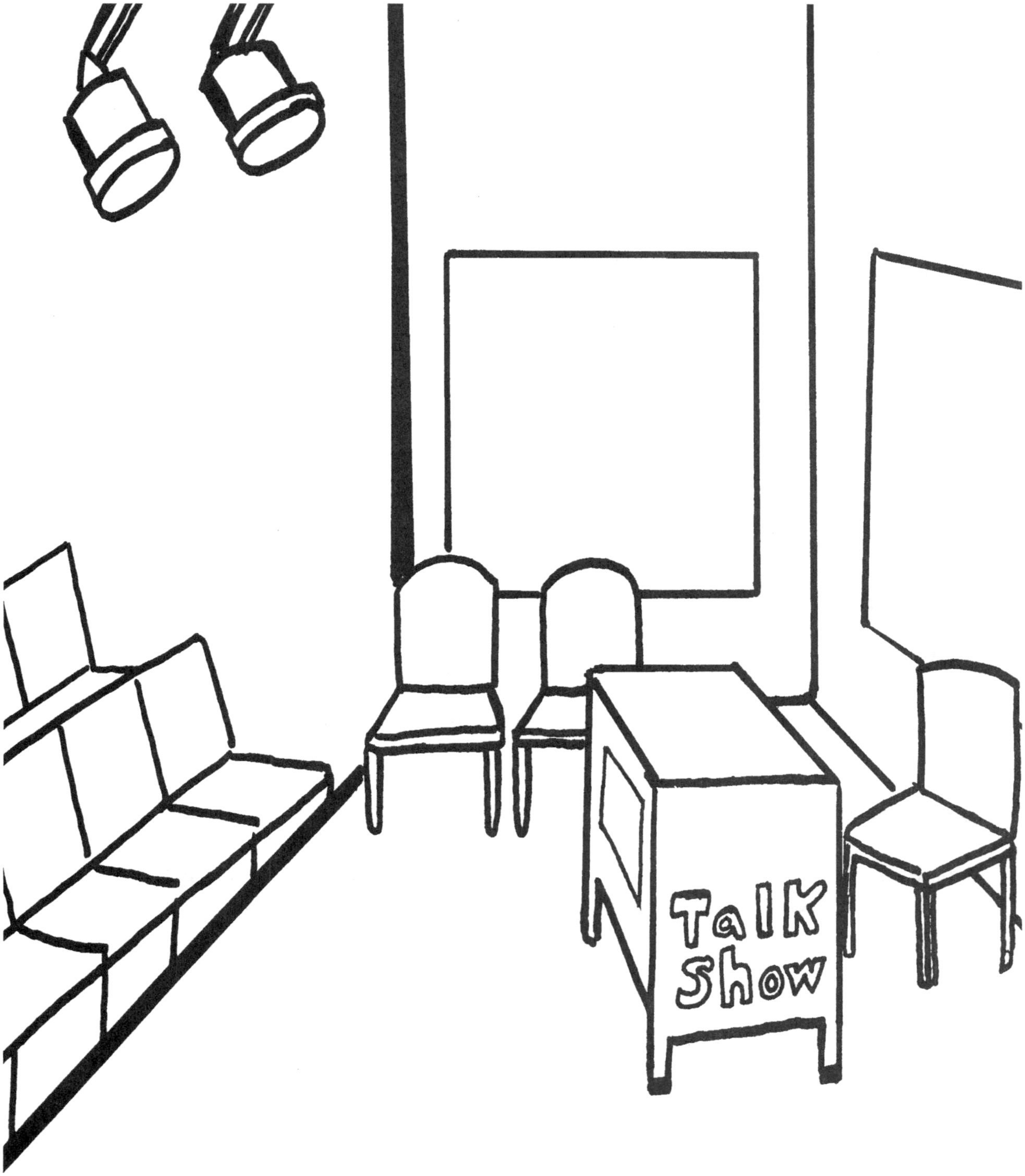

Exercise 21

THE TROPHY

Question:

Is it important for us to praise each others' achievements?

Draw or Write:

Choose three different people in your life. Decorate a trophy for each person to illustrate what they are each good at.

To Talk About:

- Describe each trophy and what it represents.
- Tell why you chose the three people to win a trophy.
- Describe a trophy someone might decorate for you.

Recommendations:

This exercise may be useful in individual sessions with children, adolescents, and adults. It may also be effective in a variety of group settings in all stages of group development.

Exercise 22

SELECT A MASK

Question:

Why is it sometimes tempting to hide our true feelings from people?

Draw or Write:

Think of some situations you may have found yourself in where you felt it necessary to hide your true feelings. Decorate each mask in a way that best illustrates how you felt in each situation.

To Talk About:

- Describe the mood and feeling connected to each mask.
- How do you think you appeared to others in each of these situations?
- Why was it necessary to hide your true feelings?

Recommendations:

This exercise may be useful in individual sessions with children, adolescents, and adults. It may also be effective in a variety of groups whose members are well acquainted with each other.

Exercise 23

MONEY CAN ONLY GO SO FAR

Question:

How does it feel when you don't have enough money for something?

Draw or Write:

In the thought bubbles, draw or write a description of how both the grownup and child feel when they can't buy the things they want.

To Talk About:

- Describe what you were communicating in each thought bubble.
- Explain why the grownup and the child might react differently about not having enough money.
- Is there any way you might help your family to save money for the extra things you might want?

Recommendations:

This exercise may be useful in individual sessions with children and adolescents.

Exercise 24

THE ONE-WAY MIRROR

Question:

What do you think it would be like to be able to look into certain places and see what was happening there?

Draw or Write:

In the picture of the one-way mirror, draw what you think might be going on inside any place you can imagine.

To Talk About:

- Describe your drawing.
- Did anything in your picture really happen?
- Describe what someone looking into a one-way mirror might see in the place where you live.

Recommendations:

This exercise may be useful in individual sessions with children, adolescents, and adults. It may also be useful in group settings in all stages of group development.

Exercise 24

Exercise 25

FEELINGS ABOUT SCHOOL

Question:

Why is it good to talk about those places at school that make kids feel frightened?

Draw or Write:

- In the picture of the school and schoolyard, color places that are scary or uncomfortable for you. (In red.)
- Color the places that make you feel safe and comfortable. (In green.)
- Color places that could go either way. (In yellow.)

To Talk About:

- Describe what happens in the places you colored red that makes you feel uncomfortable or scared.
- Why do you feel safer in the places you colored green?
- Why is it that the yellow places can go either way?
- Is there a way to change any of the (red) scary places into (green) comfortable, safe places?
- Are there any reasons why a kid would not want to share their feelings about the scary places with a grownup?

Recommendations:

This exercise may be useful in individual sessions with children and adolescents.

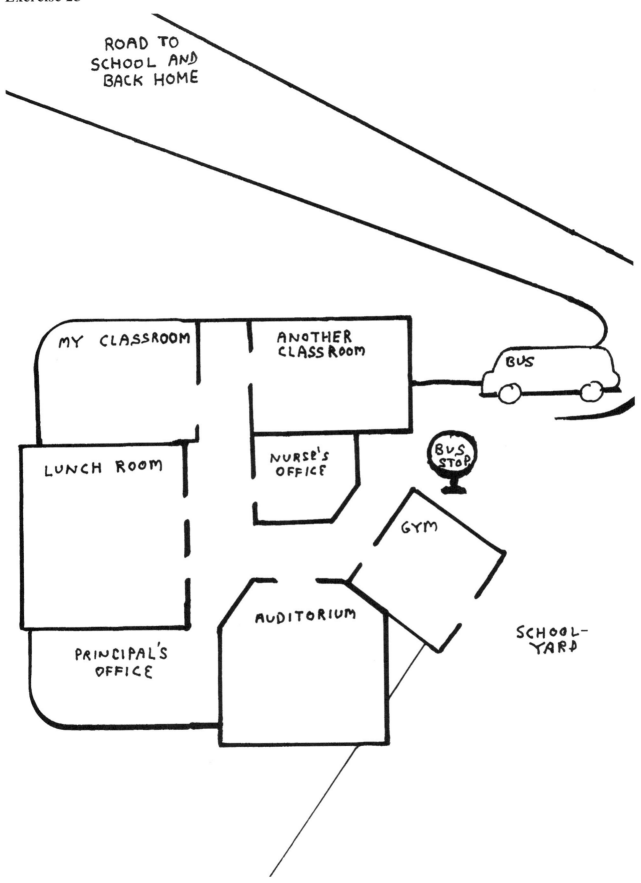

Exercise 26

THE DESERT ISLAND

Questions:

1. What is a "desert island"?
2. What feelings do you connect with the word, "stranded"?

Draw or Write:

Draw a picture of yourself and someone you definitely would not want to be stranded with on this desert island. Add anything you want to the picture to help explain what you don't like about this person.

To Talk About:

- What do you dislike about this person?
- Describe his or her personality.
- What might happen if you were alone with this person on a desert island?
- Would it be possible to change the situation in some way?

Recommendations:

This exercise may be effective in individual sessions with children, adolescents, and adults. It may also be used in group settings in the middle to later stages of development.

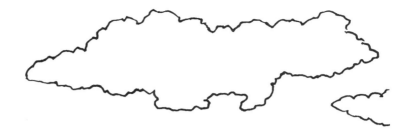

Exercise 27

THE SHOUT AND THE WHISPER

Questions:

1. When something good happens to us, why do you think you might want to tell lots of people?
2. Could there ever be a time that you would not want other people to know about something you did, or something that happened to you?

Draw or Write:

In the blank space on the megaphone, draw or write about something that happened in your life that you might want lots of people to know about. In the blank space next to the person's ear, draw or write about something in your life that you might only want to tell one person about.

To Talk About:

- What do you think people might think about what you drew or wrote about in the top picture?
- Give some of the reasons why you would not want to share the other experience with everyone.

Recommendations:

This exercise may be effective in individual sessions with children, adolescents, and adults. It may also be useful in a variety of groups whose members are well acquainted with each other.

Exercise 27

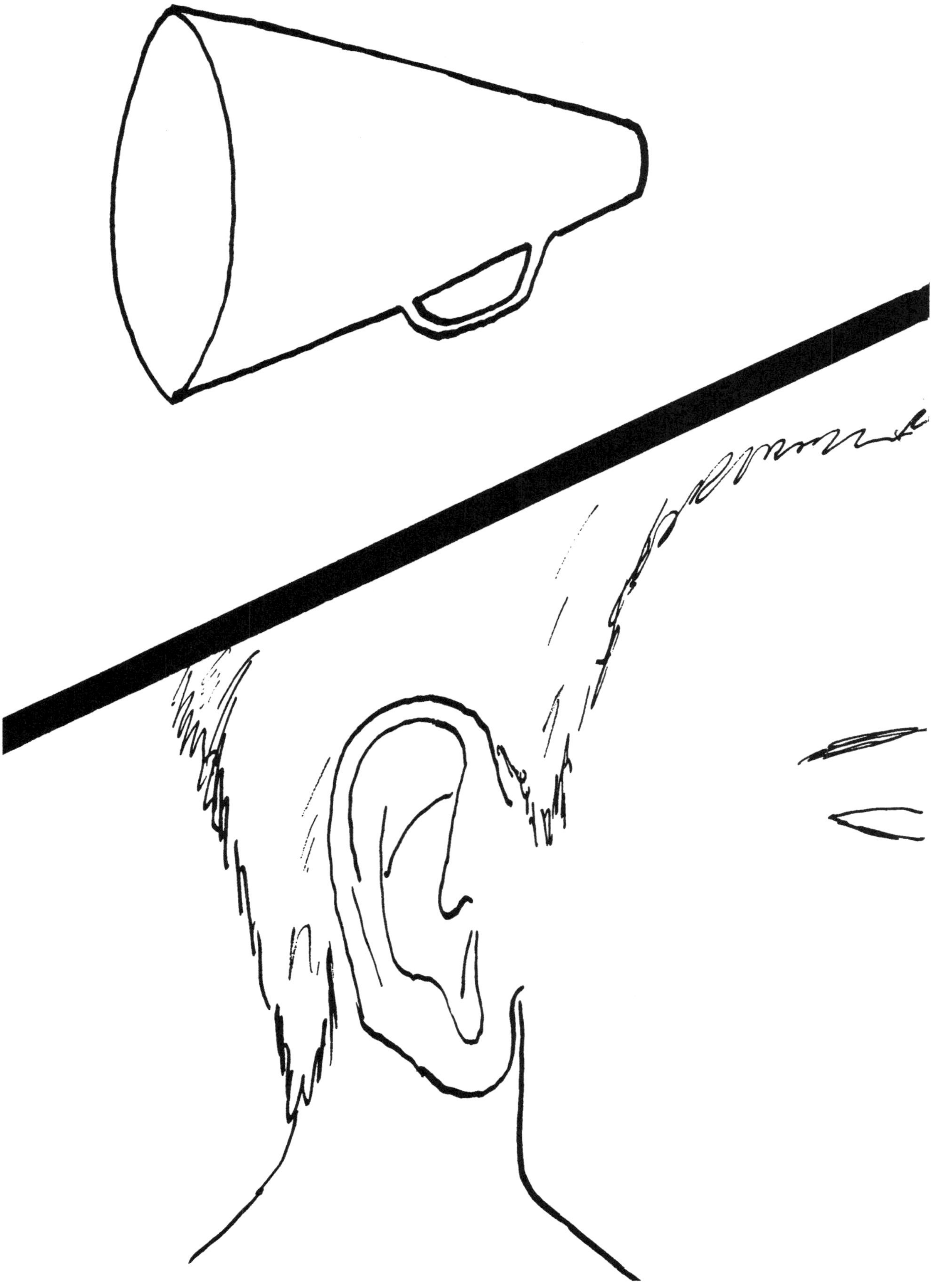

Exercise 28

WHAT SCARES US THE MOST?

Questions:

1. Do you ever feel nervous, afraid, or uncomfortable when you go someplace, or see someone, or find yourself in a certain situation?
2. Describe what happens when you feel frightened or uncomfortable.

Draw or Write:

In the blank space provided, draw or write about a person, a situation, or an experience that might have made you feel nervous, uncomfortable, or afraid.

To Talk About:

- Describe what you've written or drawn, and how you felt in that situation, or how the person or experience made you feel.
- Is there something you or someone else could have done at the time to make you feel more comfortable?
- Is there someone in your life who you feel is frightened or nervous about something?

Recommendations:

This exercise may be useful in individual sessions with children, adolescents, and adults. It may also be effective in group settings with a variety of groups in the middle to later stages of group development.

Exercise 28

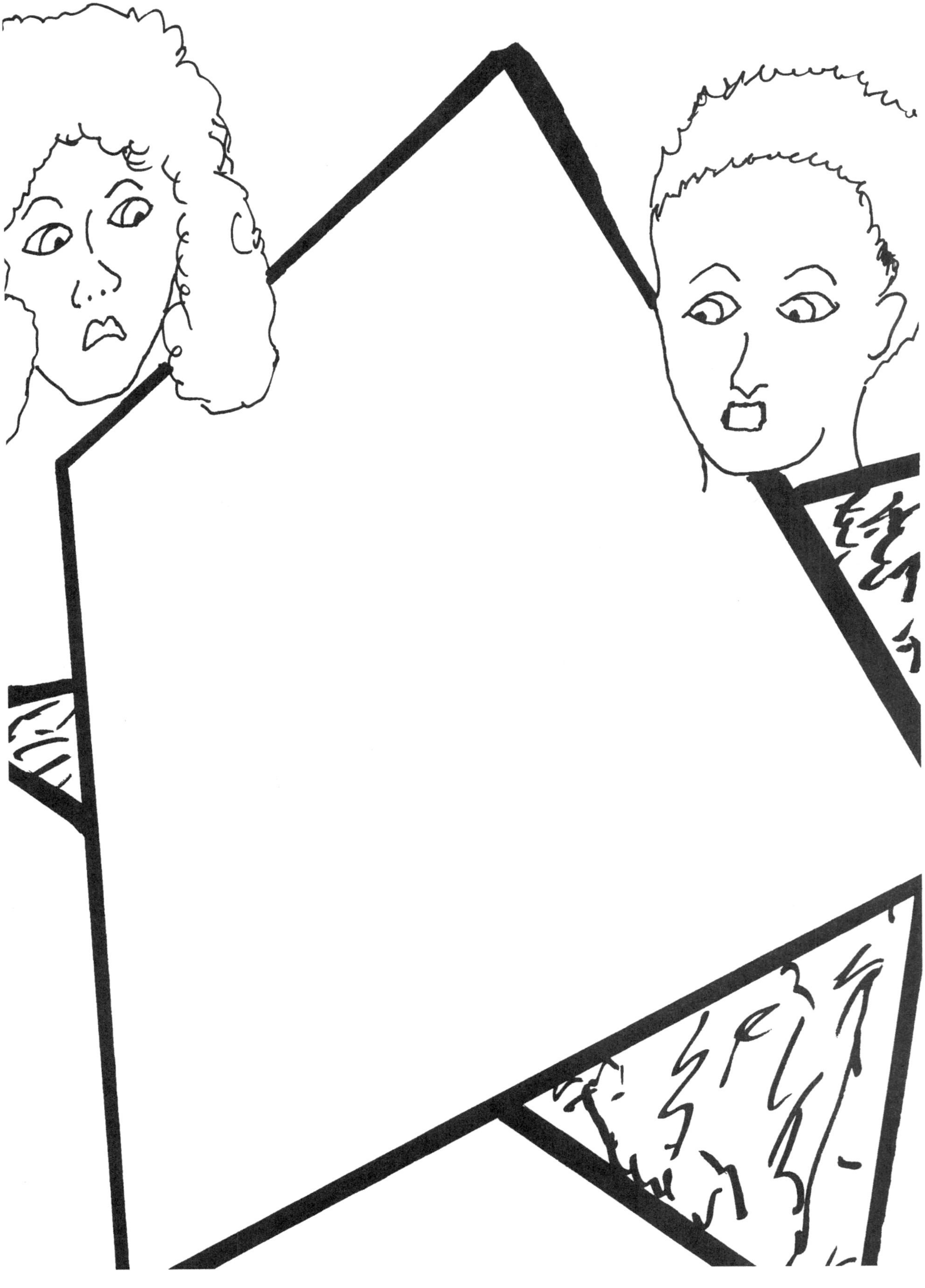

Exercise 29

A DAY TOGETHER

Question:

How does it make you feel to be with someone you really like?

Draw or Write:

In the space provided, draw in the details of a place you would like to go to with someone special. Draw in the person you would like to be with in this place. Illustrate the activity you would most enjoy sharing with this person.

To Talk About:

- What are the reasons you chose that person to spend time with?
- Why did you choose that particular activity?
- Would it add to the fun, or take away from it, if other people came along?

Recommendations:

This exercise may be useful in individual sessions with children, adolescents, and adults. It may also be effective in group settings with a variety of groups in all stages of development.

THE PEOPLE + THE PLACE
+ THE ACTIVITY =
ONE GOOD TIME

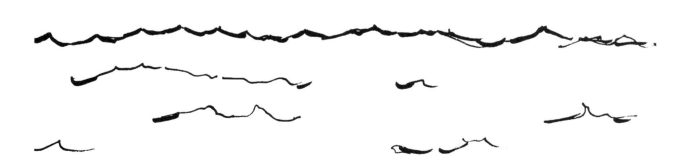

Exercise 30

THE 800-POUND GORILLA IN THE ROOM

Questions:

1. Why do people sometimes feel that they can't talk about something, and must keep it a secret?
2. What are some of the reasons it might be a good idea to talk about something being kept secret?

Draw or Write:

In the bubble above the gorilla's head, draw or write about a situation or experience that is not talked about openly, but is something everyone is aware of nevertheless. In the index card, draw or write some possible suggestions about how this situation might be resolved.

To Talk About:

- Describe the secret situation, experience, or subject you illustrated. Describe the person(s) you drew or wrote about who is(are) keeping the secret. Describe your suggestions.
- What could be the possible benefit of talking about these subjects openly and not keeping them secret anymore?

Recommendations:

This exercise may be effective in individual sessions with children, adolescents, and adults. It may also be useful in group settings with a variety of groups in the middle to later stages of development.

Exercise 31

GIVING TO OTHERS

Question:

What is the meaning of the saying, "It is better to give than to receive"?

Draw or Write:

Choose three people who you think would like to shop in each store. Write their names after "TO:". Illustrate their faces in the stores you think they would like to shop in. Next, draw the items they might like from each store. In the space marked "YOUR GIFT:" write what gift has been chosen for that person.

To Talk About:

- Why did you match these people to these stores?
- Why did you choose these people to shop for?
- How will the items you bought make these people happy?

Recommendations:

This exercise may be effective in individual sessions with children, adolescents, and adults. It may also be effective with groups in all stages of group development.

Exercise 32

A VIEW FROM THE TREE HOUSE

Question:

What are some of the things that people worry about?

Draw or Write:

In the space on the ground below the tree house, draw or write about a situation you think people might worry about and wish they could change. In the sky above the tree house, draw or write about something that could make it a better world.

To Talk About:

- Describe what you drew or wrote about.
- Talk about possible ways to change things for the better.
- Is there someone who might be able to help?
- Is there something someone could do to make it a better world for you?

Recommendations:

This exercise may be effective in individual sessions with children, adolescents, and adults. It may also be useful in groups in all stages of group development.

Exercise 32

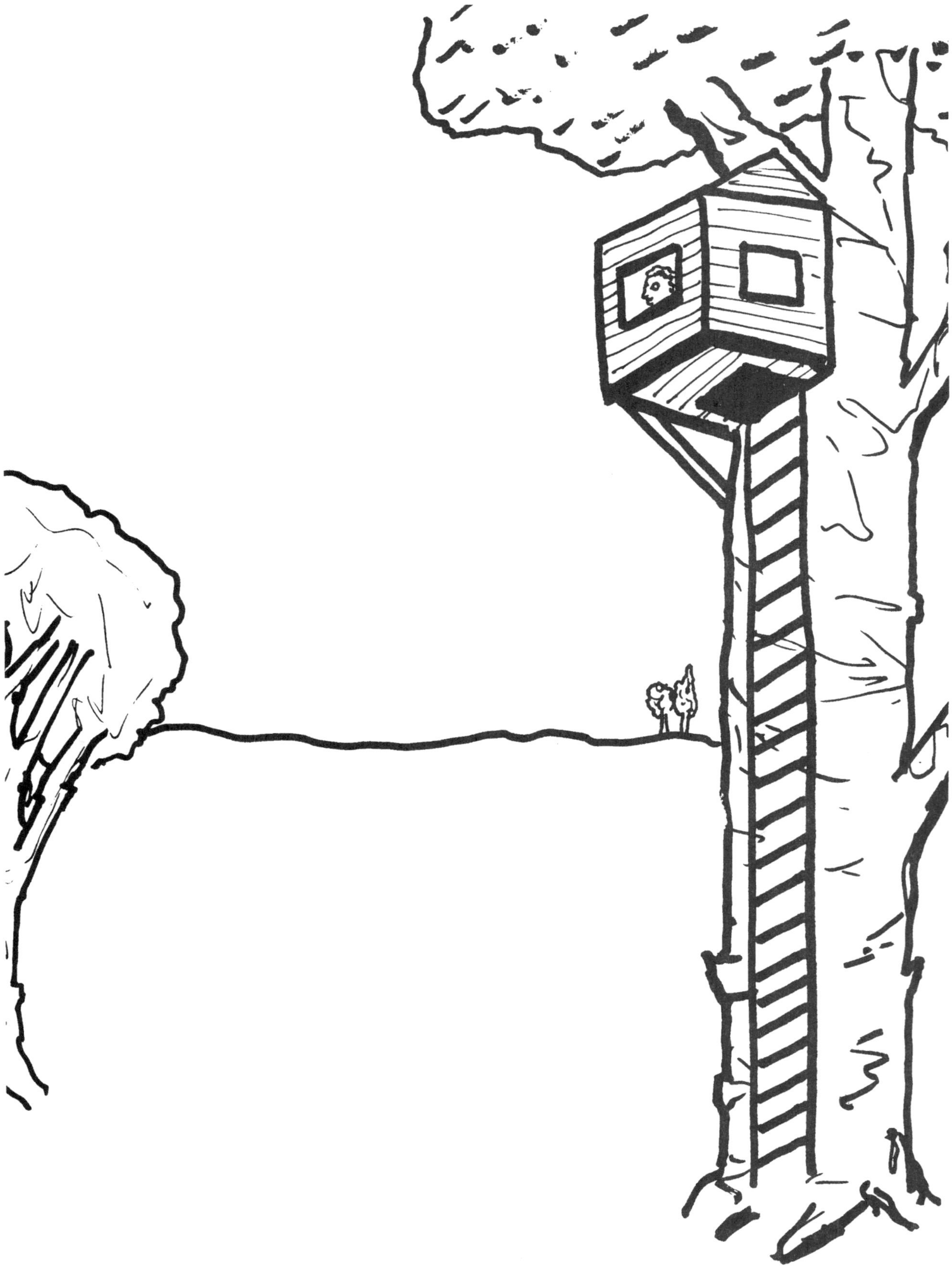

Exercise 33

TOTAL CONTROL

Question:

Can you think of some situations you would like to be in control of?

Draw or Write:

In the space above the pipes, draw or write about some situation or experience you would like to be in charge of. In the picture of the control valve, draw or write how you would handle the situation you've described. In the picture of the outcome bin, draw or write how things turned out as you wanted them to.

To Talk About:

* Describe the situation you illustrated.
* Are you having any experiences in which it might be better for others to be in control?

Recommendations:

This exercise may be effective in individual therapy with children, adolescents, and adults. It may also be useful in a variety of group settings with groups in the middle to later stages of group development.

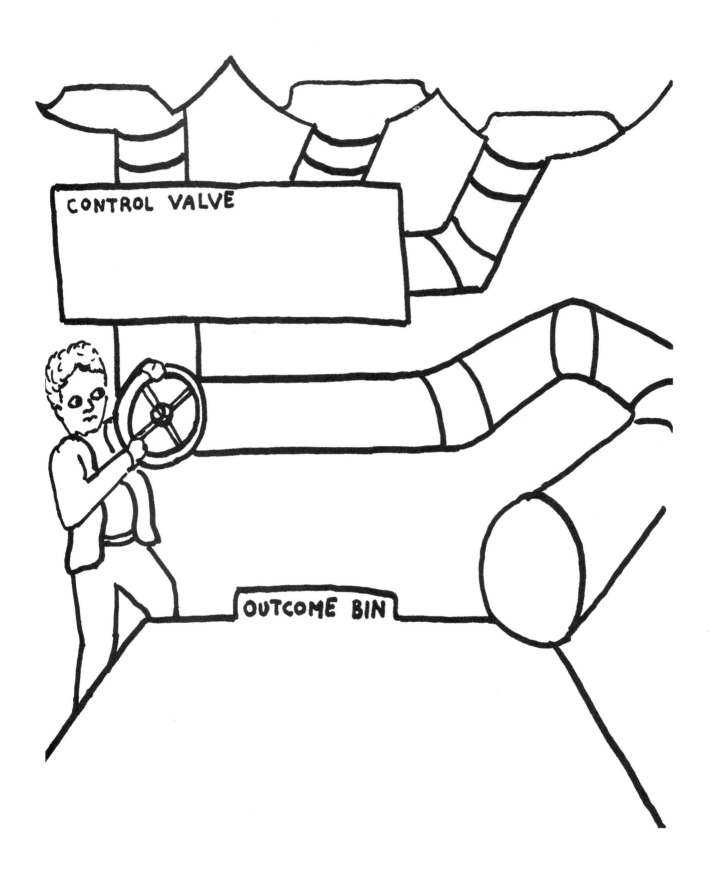

Exercise 34

THE VIDEO CAMERA

Questions:

1. What is the significance of memories?
2. How does remembering people, places, things, and events from the past make you feel?

Draw or Write:

In the space in front of the video camera, draw or write about your favorite friend, relative, teacher, or anyone else in your life. On the television screen, draw or write about favorite places, things, or events in your life.

To Talk About:

- Describe what you have drawn or written about.
- Why do they have important memories for you?
- Are there any memories from the past you want to forget?

Recommendations:

This exercise may be useful in individual sessions with children, adolescents, and adults. It may also be effective in group settings in the early stages of group development, as it is non-threatening.

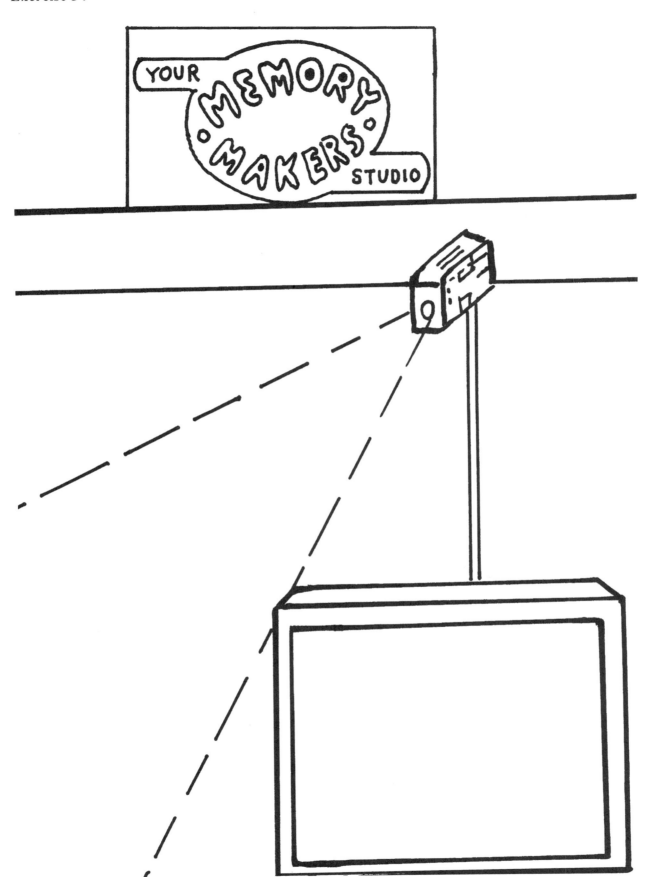

Exercise 35

ON A ROLL

Questions:

1. How does it make you feel when you try something new and it comes easily to you?
2. How do you feel when you have to really work hard at something in order to get it right?

Draw or Write:

On the rolling cart, draw or write about something you are good at and that you can do easily. On the cart that is being pushed, draw or write about something that takes a lot of effort and does not come easily to you.

To Talk About:

- Describe what you have drawn or written about.
- Why do you think it is easy for you to do what you illustrated on the rolling cart?
- How do you feel when you see others being able to do certain things easily, when you yourself have a hard time doing them?
- Is there something you can do to make the difficult things easier?
- Is there someone you would like to ask for help with those things?

Recommendations:

This exercise may be useful in individual sessions with children, adolescents, and adults. It may also be effective in a variety of group settings, with groups in the middle to later stages of development.

Exercise 36

THE DINNER OF A LIFETIME

Question:

What does it mean to be the host or hostess of a fancy dinner party?

Draw or Write:

In the space on the plates, illustrate the food you would choose to serve. Around the table, draw in a few of the guests you might invite to your party. Complete the sentences on the menu, the invitation list, and the word balloon and banner.

To Talk About:

- Why did you choose these people to come to dinner?
- What could you do to help your guests get along with each other?
- What do you think your guests might talk about at your party?

Recommendations:

This exercise may be useful in individual sessions with children, adolescents, and adults. It may also be effective in a variety of group settings with members in all stages of group development.

Exercise 37

HONEST FEEDBACK

Question:

Can you describe people you know who have different kinds of personalities?

Draw or Write:

In each picture card, match each figure with someone you know. In the blank space below the picture cards, illustrate your own personality.

To Talk About:

- Describe how each type of personality sometimes makes you feel.
- Describe your own personality.
- What are some of the ways different people react to you?

Recommendations:

This exercise may be useful in individual sessions with children, adolescents, and adults. It may also be effective in a variety of groups whose members are well acquainted with one another.

Exercise 38

THE SCHOOLYARD HERO

Question:

Was there ever a time during school when you wished you had a real Superhero to help you handle certain situations involving others?

Draw or Write:

In the blank space in front of the school, draw or write about a situation or experience you might need help with. In the blank space on the cape, draw or write how that hero could help you, without the use of violence or physical force.

To Talk About:

- Describe your illustrations.
- Why is it better to find solutions to problems without fighting?
- Is there anyone you know who you think might benefit from talking about something bothering them, or about a problem they may be having?

Recommendations:

This exercise may be effective in individual sessions with children and adolescents.

Exercise 39

WHO SPILLED THE BEANS?

Question:

What does the word "trust" mean to you?

Draw or Write:

In the empty space near the spilled beans, draw or write about a situation where you or someone else were trusted to keep something secret, but instead told others.

To Talk About:

- Describe the situation you illustrated.
- What happened when the secret was told?
- How were other people affected by this?
- If the situation happened again, would you do anything differently?
- Are there any situations that should never be kept secret, but always told to someone else?

Recommendations:

This exercise may be useful in individual sessions with children, adolescents, and adults. It may also be effective in a variety of group settings where members are in the middle to later stages of development.

Exercise 40

I'M REALLY ANGRY

Questions:

1. What are some of the things that make you angry?
2. What happens when you get angry?

Draw or Write:

In the empty space below the person's head, draw or write about something that made you very mad. This can be anything from the past, or a recent experience.

To Talk About:

- Describe what you illustrated.
- What were some of the reasons this made you so angry?
- How did you react when you felt this anger?
- If the situation were to happen again, how would you react this time?

Recommendations:

This exercise may be useful in individual sessions with children, adolescents, and adults. It may also be effective in group settings that are in the middle to later stage of group development and which have developed some degree of trust between members.

Exercise 41

RECIPE FOR FRIENDSHIP

Questions:

1. What makes a good friend?
2. Can you describe some of the reasons you would consider someone a good friend?

Draw or Write:

In the space marked "main dishes," illustrate someone in your life you consider a good friend. In the space below, where something has spilled, illustrate anyone you feel has not been a good friend. On the recipe page, complete the ingredients for a good friendship.

To Talk About:

- What is there about the person you illustrated that makes him or her a good friend?
- Why do you think the other person is not a good friend?
- Is there something about you that makes you someone's good friend?
- Is there anyone you would like to get to know better?

Recommendations:

This exercise may be useful in individual sessions with children, adolescents, and adults. It may also be effective in a variety of group settings with groups in all stages of development.

MAIN DISHES

RECIPE FOR
FRIENDSHIP

1½ cups of

2 cups of

6 teaspoons of

1 pound of

dash of

generous portion of

Exercise 42

PROBLEM-SOLVING SKILLS

Question:

What does it mean to have problem-solving skills?

Draw or Write:

Think of a difficult situation you or someone else may have encountered, and draw or write about it to the left of the illustrated book. In the book itself, illustrate some of the skills you think might be needed to deal with the problems you describe.

To Talk About:

- Describe the situation and some of the problem-solving skills you illustrated.
- How did everything turn out?
- Is the situation you described actually happening now?

Recommendations:

This exercise may be effective in individual sessions with children, adolescents, and adults. It may also be useful in a variety of group settings with groups in all stages of development.

Exercise 43

THE VIEW FROM MY ROOM

Question:

Who are some of the people in your life?

Draw or Write:

In the space inside the drawing of the window, draw or write about some of the people you live with, or people who visit frequently.

To Talk About:

- Describe the people you illustrated and their different personalities.
- How do they get along with each other?
- Are there times when you would like to see them relate in a different way to each other?
- How do these people get along with you?

Recommendations:

This exercise may be useful in individual sessions with children, adolescents, and adults. It may also be effective in a variety of group settings with groups in all stages of development.

Exercise 44

WELL DONE!

Questions:

1. How does it make you feel when someone appreciates and values something you do?
2. What are some of the ways people show their appreciation?

Draw or Write:

In the space above the people giving the "high five," draw or write about something you did that was appreciated by someone else. Illustrate the person or people who valued what you did. In the space below, draw or write about something special you did that was not valued or appreciated by others.

To Talk About:

- Why do you think no one noticed or appreciated what you did?
- Was anyone around who should have given you praise, but did not?
- Why do you think that happened?

Recommendations:

This exercise may be effective in individual sessions with children, adolescents, and adults, as well as groups in all stages of group development.

Exercise 45

KEEPING OUR DISTANCE

Question:

Are there times when you might feel you want to avoid certain people or situations in your life?

Draw or Write:

In the space to the right of the village, draw or write about something or someone you wish you could avoid.

To Talk About:

- Describe what you drew or wrote about.
- Give the reasons you'd like to avoid the situation or person(s) you have illustrated.
- Tell why avoiding them seems so difficult.
- Are there any new strategies you could use to stay away from the people or situation you described?
- Is there someone who could help you do this?

Recommendations:

This exercise may be useful in individual sessions with children, adolescents, and adults. It may also be effective in group settings with group members in the middle to later stages of development.

Exercise 45

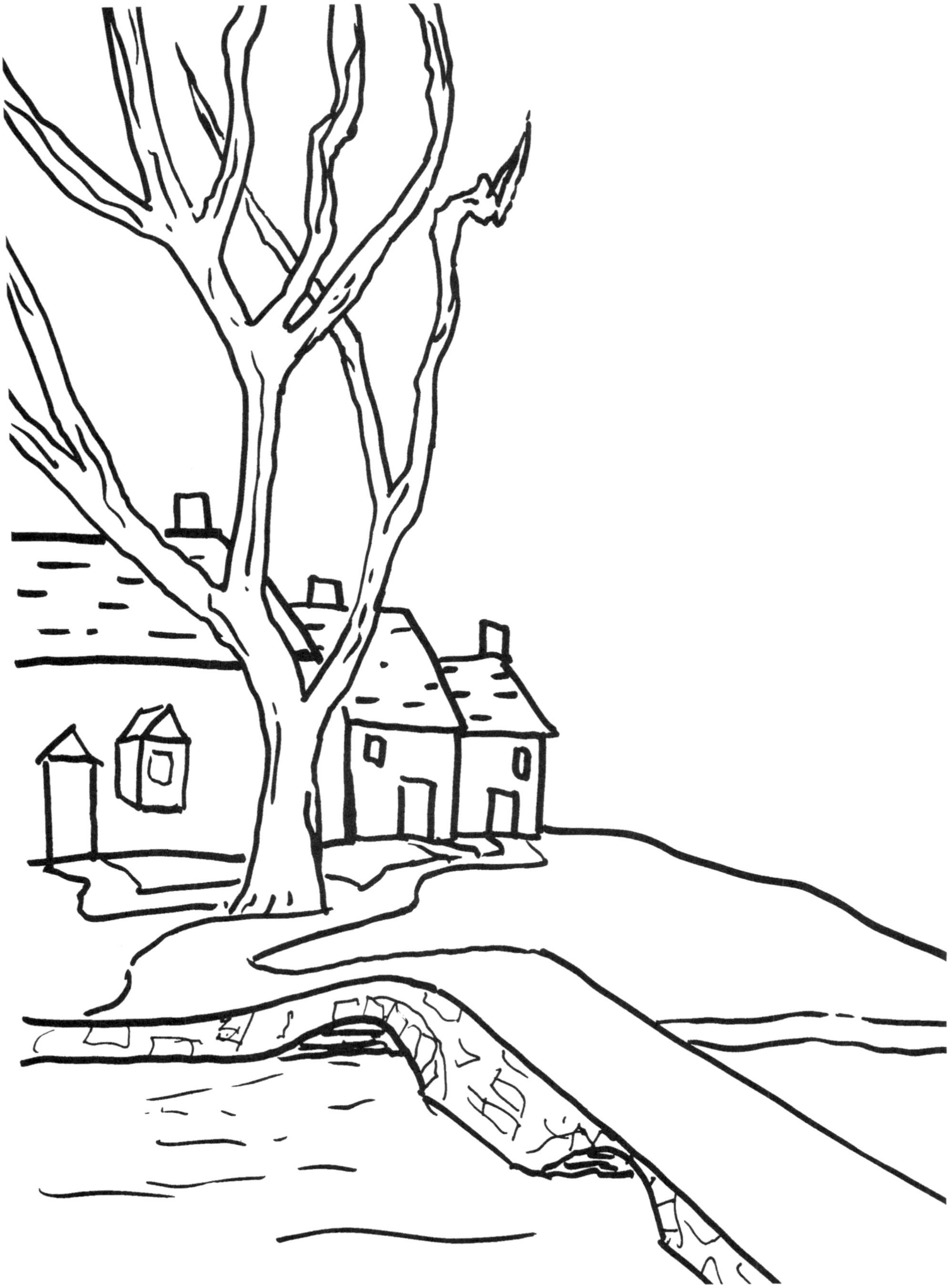

Exercise 46

THE BLINDFOLD

Question:

Can you think of any situations where it seemed that people had blindfolds on and were not aware that someone needed their help?

Draw or Write:

On the picture of the blindfold, draw or write about a situation where someone needed help in some way and other people were not aware of it.

To Talk About:

- Describe your illustration.
- Why do you think other people were not aware that the person needed help?
- Did you ever feel like you needed help in some way, but people were ignoring you?
- Can you suggest ways to deal with feelings of being ignored or not being understood?

Recommendations:

This exercise may be useful in individual sessions with children, adolescents, and adults. It may also be useful in group settings with a variety of groups in all stages of group development.

Exercise 47

THE WINNING TICKET

Question:

Did you ever have a chance to win a prize in a contest?

Draw or Write:

On one blank ticket, draw a picture of something you would wish to win. On the other ticket, draw a prize for someone in your life.

To Talk About:

- Describe what you won and what you liked about it.
- Why did you choose a particular prize for that other person?
- How should people react when they win a prize they don't like?

Recommendations:

This exercise may be effective in individual sessions with children, adolescents, and adults. It may also be used in a variety of group settings in all stages of development.

Exercise 48

BIG TROUBLE AHEAD

Question:

How does it make you feel when unexpected problems arise?

Draw or Write:

In the thought bubble above the roller coaster going up the hill, draw or write about a possible problem or difficult situation you think might happen in the future. In the thought bubble to the right of the roller coaster going down the hill, draw or write how you might deal with the problem as it happens. In the thought bubble at the end of the ride, draw or write how you might feel if you had to go through this experience.

To Talk About:

- Describe your illustrations.
- What are some reasons you think the problem you described might occur?
- Is there anything negative someone else is doing now that seems to ensure that this problem will actually occur?

Recommendations:

This exercise may be useful in individual sessions with children, adolescents, and adults. It may also be useful in group settings in all stages of development.

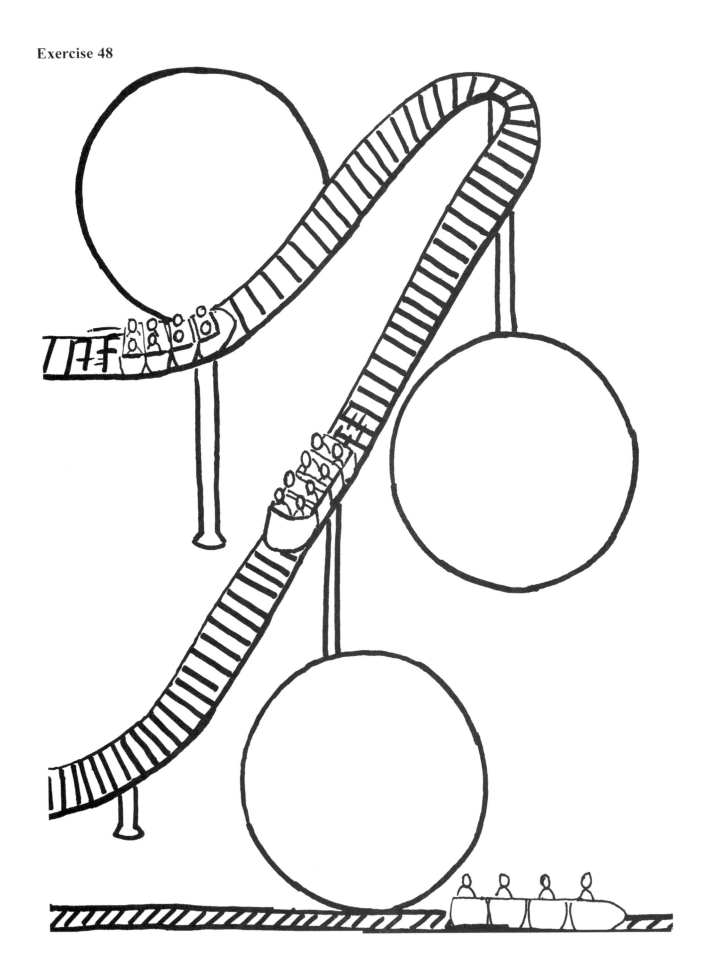

Exercise 49

THE OPPOSITE MAN

Questions:

1. Is it ever possible for there to be a good side to a seemingly bad situation?
2. Can you give any examples of situations you thought would be bad for you, but actually turned out to be good?

Draw or Write:

In the space above the thumbs down part of the picture, draw or write about a situation or experience you thought would be bad for you. In the space below the thumbs up portion of the picture, draw or write how the same experience or situation turned out to be good for you.

To Talk About:

- Describe what you illustrated.
- Why do you think this situation had both good and bad aspects to it?
- Do some people have trouble seeing both sides of a situation?

Recommendations:

This exercise may be effective in individual sessions with children, adolescents, and adults. It may also be useful in a variety of group settings with groups in all stages of development.

Exercise 49

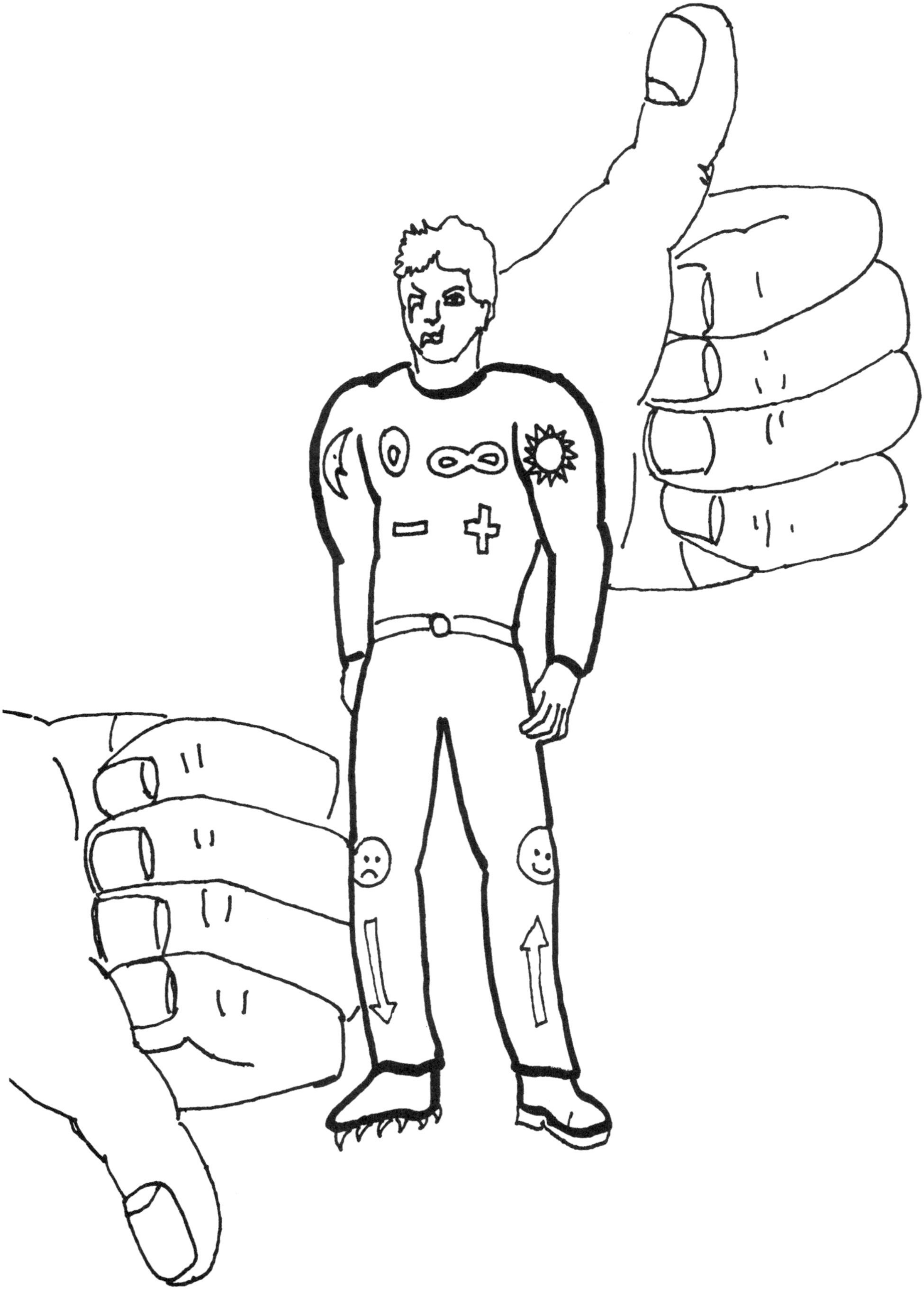

Exercise 50

THE GARDEN

Questions:

1. Can you describe a problem you have been concerned with?
2. Is there something you or someone else did to make this problem worse?
3. Are there times when a bad experience can be made better because of something positive you or someone else might do?

Draw or Write:

Above the picture of the man watering the weeds, draw or describe how a problem you had was made even worse by something you or someone else did, or failed to do. Above the picture of the man planting the seeds, draw or write what you or someone else might do to make a bad experience better.

To Talk About:

- Describe the problem you illustrated. How did you or someone else make this problem worse?
- How do you think the problem should have been dealt with?
- Is there anything you would like to do for someone else to help them with a problem?

Recommendations:

This exercise may be useful with children, adolescents, and adults. It may also be effective in a variety of groups whose members are well acquainted with one another.

WATERING OUR WEEDS

PLANTING NEW SEEDS

Exercise 51

GONE BUT NOT FORGOTTEN

Question:

Can you describe someone or something that you miss? These can include friends, family members, pets, favorite places, and fun times that are gone.

Draw or Write:

In the blank space provided, draw or write about some things that you miss.

To Talk About:

- Describe your illustration.
- Talk about your memories and why they are important to you.
- Is there anything anyone can do to help you feel better about your feelings of loss?

Recommendations:

This exercise may be effective in individual sessions with children, adolescents, and adults. It may also be useful in group sessions in all stages of group development.

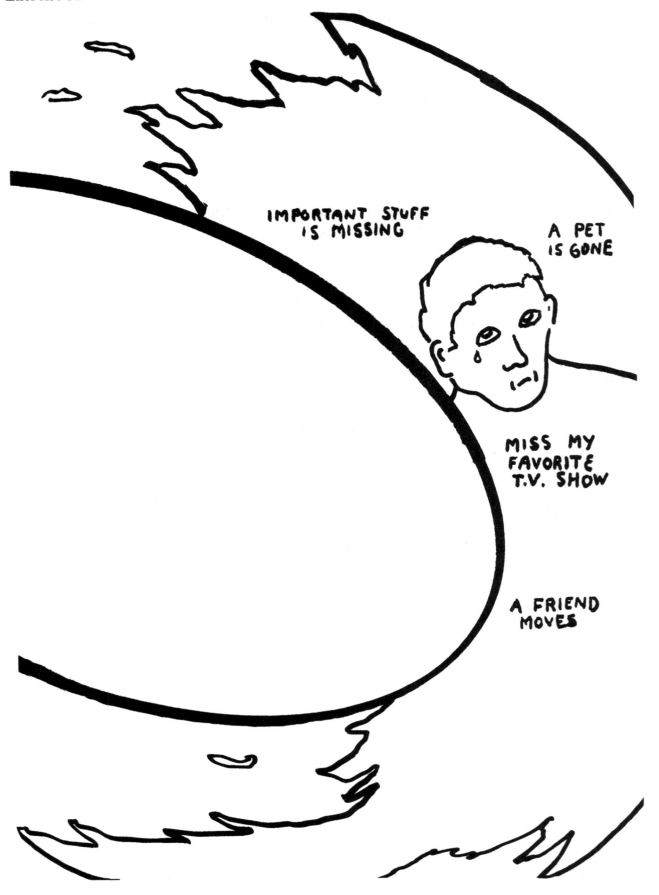

Exercise 52

THE ANONYMOUS LETTER

Question:

Did you ever want to tell someone something but not want them to know it was coming from you?

Draw or Write:

Pretend you are sending a letter to someone without signing your name. On the illustrated computer screen, draw or write what you want to tell someone.

To Talk About:

- Identify the person you chose to write to.
- Why did you choose that person?
- Describe why it might be too difficult to speak to the person directly.
- Are there times when it might be best not to tell people what you are really thinking?

Recommendations:

This exercise may be effective in individual sessions with children, adolescents, and adults. It may also be effective with a wide variety of groups whose members are well acquainted with each other.

Exercise 52

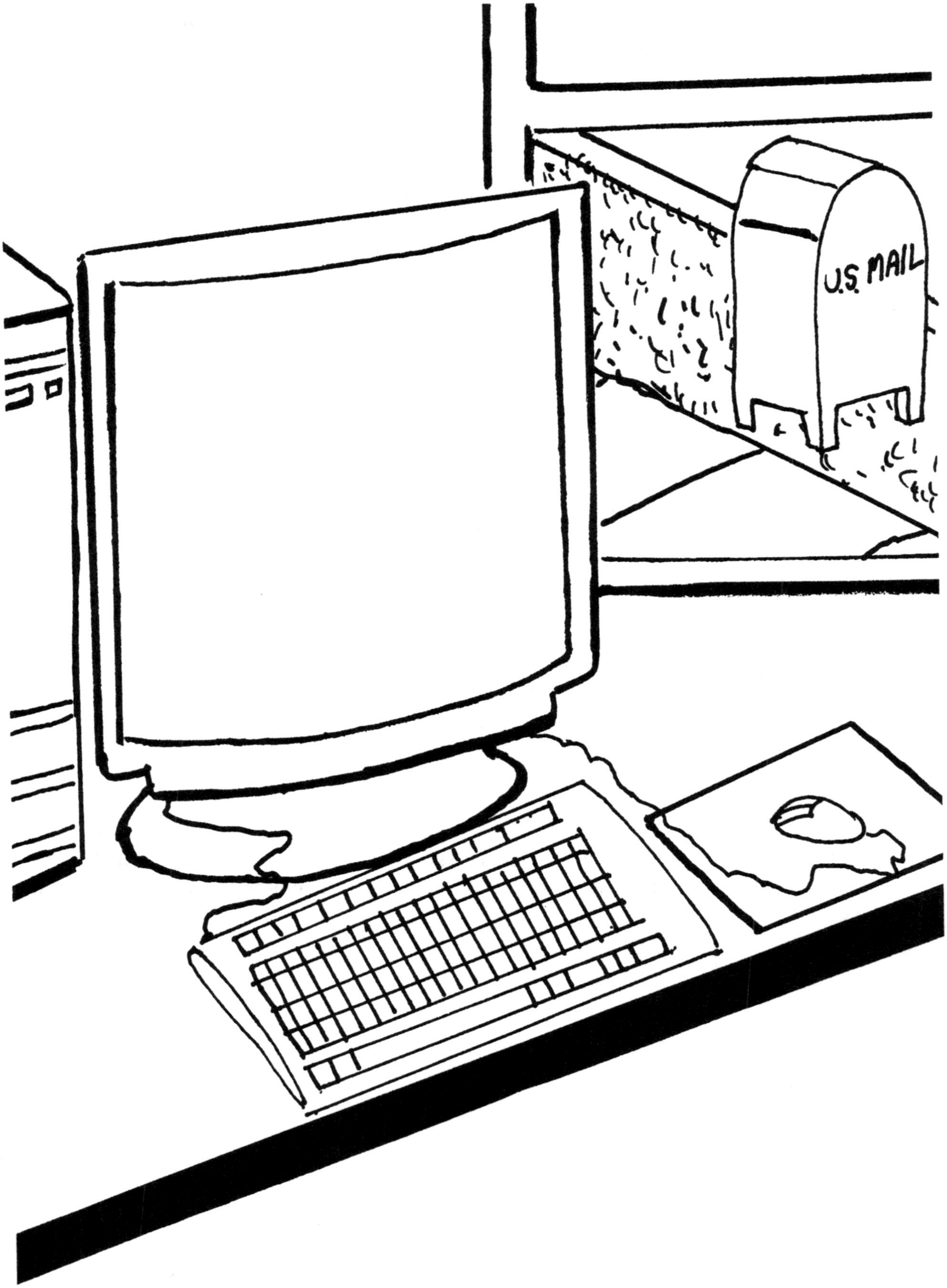

More Titles For Those Who Work With Groups

Creative Therapy I
Jane Dossick & Eugene Shea
Item Code - CT   124 pp.   1988   0-943158-50-8

Creative Therapy II
Jane Dossick & Eugene Shea
Item Code - CT2   118 pp.   1990   0-943158-60-5

Creative Therapy III
Jane Dossick & Eugene Shea
Item Code - CT3   116 pp.   1995   1-56887-008-6

**Creative Therapy: 52 Exercises
for Individuals and Groups**
Jane Dossick & Eugene Shea
Item Code - CT4   118 pp.   2006   1-56887-103-1

**Filial Therapy: Strengthening
Parent-Child Relationships
Through Play (Second Edition)**
Risë VanFleet
Item Code - FT2   90 pp.   2005   1-56887-090-6

**Group Therapy: An Integrative
Cognitive Social-Learning Approach**
Robert Henley Woody
Item Code - GTIA   172 pp.   2004   1-56887-088-4

**Group Exercises for Enhancing
Social Skills and Self-Esteem**
SiriNam S. Khalsa
Item Code - GEE   150 pp.   1996   1-56887-020-5

**Group Exercises for Enhancing
Social Skills and Self-Esteem (Volume 2)**
SiriNam S. Khalsa
Item Code - GEE2   156 pp.   1999   1-56887-056-6

**Group Interventions & Exercises for
Enhancing Children's Communication,
Cooperation, & Confidence**
Melissa E. DeRosier
Item Code - GIE   136 pp.   2002   1-56887-075-2

**Group Work With Elders: 50 Therapeutic Exercises
for Reminiscence, Validation, and Remotivation**
Ann L. Link
Item Code - GWW   140 pp.   1997   1-56887-030-2

**How to Design, Develop, and
Market Health Care Seminars**
Ronald J. Friedman & Penny Altman
Item Code - HDD   224 pp.   1997   1-56887-029-9

Learning to Master Your Chronic Pain
(Patient Handbook & CD-ROM)
Robert N. Jamison
Handbook Item Code - MCPW   230 pp.   1996   1-56887-019-1
CD-ROM Item Code - MCPCD   1997   1-56887-034-5
Handbook & CD-ROM Item Code - MCPAK

**Mastering Chronic Pain: A Professional's
Guide to Behavioral Treatment**
(Therapist Manual)
Robert N. Jamison
Item Code - MCP   192 pp.   1996   1-56887-018-3

**Structured Adolescent
Psychotherapy Groups**
Billie Farmer Corder
Item Code - SAPG   164 pp.   1994   0-943158-74-5

**Structured Psychotherapy Groups
for Sexually Abused Children and
Adolescents**
Billie Farmer Corder
Item Code - SCA   272 pp.   2000   1-56887-058-2

**Therapeutic Exercises for Children:
Guided Self-Discovery Using
Cognitive-Behavioral Techniques**
(Workbook)
*Robert D. Friedberg, Barbara A. Friedberg,
& Rebecca J. Friedberg*
Item Code - TCW   154 pp.   2001   1-56887-065-5

**Therapeutic Exercises for Children:
Professional Guide**
Robert D. Friedberg & Lori E. Crosby
Item Code - TC   140 pp.   2001   1-56887-064-7

**Therapeutic Exercises for
Victimized and Neglected Girls:
Applications for Individual,
Family, & Group Psychotherapy**
Pearl Berman
Item Code - TEV   178 pp.   1994   1-56887-003-5

If You Found This Book Useful . . .

You might want to know more about our other titles.

For a complete listing of publications, please send us the following information. You may fold this sheet to make a postpaid reply envelope. If you ordered this book from Professional Resource Press, your name is already on our preferred customer mailing list and you do not need to return this form to receive future catalogs.

Name _____
Please Print

Address _____

Address _____

City/State/Zip _____ This is my ❏ home   ❏ office

Telephone (____)_____ Fax (____)_____ Email _____

I am a: ____ Psychologist   ____ Clinical Social Worker   ____ Marriage and Family Therapist   ____ Mental Health Counselor
        ____ School Psychologist   ____ Psychiatrist   ____ Other (please describe)_____

CT4/8/06

Please fold on this line and the solid line below, tape (DO NOT STAPLE), and mail.

Please fold on this line and the solid line above, tape (DO NOT STAPLE), and mail.

_____

_____

_____

Affix
Postage
Here

PROFESSIONAL RESOURCE PRESS
PO BOX 15560
SARASOTA FL 34277-1560

NOTES

NOTES

NOTES

NOTES